T0129331

Pathway
to
Freedom

In Pursuit of Liberty

J. Monroe

Order this book online at www.trafford.com
or email orders@trafford.com

Most Trafford titles are also available at major online book retailers.

Printed in the United States of America.

ISBN: 978-1-4669-1163-5 (sc)
ISBN: 978-1-4669-1162-8 (hc)
ISBN: 978-1-4669-1161-1 (e)

Library of Congress Control Number: 2012902474

Trafford rev. 03/01/2012

 www.trafford.com

North America & international
toll-free: 1 888 232 4444 (USA & Canada)
phone: 250 383 6864 ♦ fax: 812 355 4082

Contents

Dedications

For Anita, Bernard and Kathleen, John, and so many others for whom without their unwavering encouragements, unconditional faith and friendship, this project may never have been accomplished.

To the Men and Women of The United States Armed Forces, both the fallen, and those who carry the fight for Freedom, we each are forever indebted.

Introduction

"I predict future Happiness for Americans if they can prevent the government from wasting the labors of the people under the pretense of taking care of them." –Thomas Jefferson.

Pathway to Freedom presents a minimalistic approach to both ends.

With emphasis on self-education, Pathway to Freedom meets the needs of today's hurry-scurry lifestyle.

If Democracy and Freedom is to survive, the citizens of the United States must better acquaint themselves with both principles and functions of Freedoms and government. Only through increased individual knowledge of the Constitution, Freedoms granted, and the appropriate methods of limiting an ever expanding government, can Democracy and Freedom of America survive.

More important than having an answer, is knowing where to locate the answer.

Exploring the Constitution

Not intended as an in-depth, line-by-line study, but rather a guide, *Pathway to Freedom* introduces citizens to basic interpretative methods and understandings and of the Constitution of the United States.

Contrasting more than a century of "controlled knowledge" through manipulative education, the Constitution presents less difficulty of understanding than educational communities and political power mongers would have you accept.

The naturalized citizenship program presents a prime example of the ease of understanding the Constitution and basic governmental functions. If an immigrant who speaks no English or given the opportunity can study the several courses, learn English, then pass the citizenship test in five years, certainly an interested citizen can accomplish as much.

Exploring the Constitution will prove easy for some, while difficult for those farther removed from classrooms. Once abandoned, study habits are difficult to re-establish, so try this simple approach:

1. Set aside at least hour each day for study;
2. Avoid interruptions; and, above all, relax and enjoy your enlightenments.

Armed with only three key ingredients, the average lay-person can study and understand as much as 70% of the Constitution in as little as three months. Mindset, education, and time will provide astonishing results.

Mindset: Paramount to mindset is the originality of the document. What the words actually present in meaning, as opposed to what one wishes to insert as interpretation.

One must consider the backgrounds, various educational levels, personal convictions, and political attitudes of not only the writers of the Constitution, but of the many state-level individuals who ratified the document. No political agenda is sanctioned, promoted, or served, by the Constitution, therefore, clearing the mind of all previous political influence is crucial to clear understandings of the document.

Essential to an objective mind is the recognition and acceptance of the purpose of the Constitution and the Democratic Republic of the United States. The Constitution is the foundational document of only one nation and one society. Multiple races, cultures, and religious faiths are considered and provided for, within the Constitution of the United States. Not the world, but One, Independent Nation, and its citizens.

If one can accept this mindset, the remainder is only a matter of perseverance.

Education: An eleventh grade high school education is sufficient. The most important aspect is a thorough knowledge of punctuation and sentence structure. With no writing aids available, it was common practice in the eighteenth century to write in multiple compound sentences. Thereby, considerably more commas, colons, and semi-colons were used than in modern literature. Many varying thoughts and subjects were interconnected through the use of commas, colons, and semi-colons. Extreme care must be taken in order to discern correctness. Too, while definitions remain unchanged, some words common to the era are no longer used.

Reading for knowledge: Most crucial of all, is the time spent reading and studying the Constitution. An entirely new dimension of reading-for-knowledge must be acquired.

The Constitution is a guideline, a successive extension of interactive, and interconnecting elements. No phrase, no subject, is without interactivity with one or more elements. Therefore, approach the Constitution with a minimum of four distinctive readings.

First reading: Relax and read lightly to let the mind assess the continuity. Do not try to make notes or remember specific topics.

Second reading: Relax but be more attentive to each of the separate elements while noting their inactive connections.

Third reading: Begin to take notes on topics of individual interests, stopping when a similar topic is found. Note and assess the connections.

Fourth reading: It is here that you should begin the individual analysis of interconnections to the overall continuity.

In written words, the Constitution establishes three branches of government. While each are somewhat complex in understanding, study will provide an individual sufficient knowledge of each.

Of paramount importance is the contextual Fourth Branch of Government. From the opening statement, to its closure, the Constitution illustrates "We The People" as the Fourth, unnamed, yet ultimate authority of the United States Government.

Take advantage of all reference materials. Although the Constitution stands as the governing document, its predecessors, The Articles of Confederation and Declaration of Independence, must not be dismissed. Many items of the early documents were incorporated into the Constitution. It is those items that add support and clarity to the current Constitution. To fail to reference these documents, is to fail to accurately interpret the final Constitution. The better informed the voting public, the more successful the preservations of Democracy, Freedom, Individual Rights and Liberties.

Rights by Choice

Of the Constitutions of Free Nations of the world, only the Constitution of The United States stands without political influence or affiliation. The U.S. Constitution provides more "**Choices**" and fewer **restraints** than any other. Each are needed for self-governing, yet when imbalanced and abused, the same allows for loss of Democracy, failure of government, and destruction of individual rights and liberties!

An estimated 35% of our nations' population is now active in attempts to change our form of government! Lack of understanding of subject-matter tends to induce another 35% into these non-democratic actions! As Constitution, Democracy, Freedoms, Rights, Liberties, Justice, and similar cries are heard across the nation and around the world, perhaps as Free people, it is time Americans re-evaluate choices and convictions.

Rights and Liberties are choices, being neither demands or restraints. A right is an individual choice to be decided, either to exercise or not. You have no right to make a choice on behalf of, or impose your choices on, another citizen. No better tool of Rights assessment can be found than the Constitution of the United States!

The Constitution provides an outline of two elementary agendas: 1.) That of a free people to self-govern through debate and compromise; or, use the same outline as a road map to self-destruction; and, 2.) limited powers of a governing body.

Checks and balances of both restraints and **choices** are exemplified throughout the Constitution, the first being found in the process of selecting officials. Irrespective of political affiliation, nationality, racial, religious, or ethnic group, the rule of "rule by majority" defines voter-majority only, the larger portion of the whole, and the lesser portion, respectively.—The only racial separations were defeated by the Fourteenth Amendment and successive acts of Congress addressing Native American Indians.

The Constitution demands rule of the majority. If we adhere to this premise, we notice a compromise in abstract individual rights. At times it seems, we are doing all the "giving" while others are "taking." Yet over time, we learn that our time of receiving arrives and others are on the "giving" end. The Founders recognized, and placed effective, acceptable compromises as opposed to a direct democratic system.

When we consider individual rights, we must recognize among millions there is no such item as "individual rights unquestioned." The Constitutional dictate is that "no citizen" be denied rights "without due process."—Through elected officials, special interest groups, and ourselves, we choose whether or not, and when or not, to allow or disallow "due process." Again, we have a choice between dominance—non-democratic actions—or democracy through compromise!

Education, a subject addressed only minimally through legislated law, is a most profound choice! Mandated education to the minimum age of sixteen is a protective device, preventing citizens from entering adulthood totally amiss of basic skills of survival in the business world.—Beyond the mandated education, we still have choices! We can either accept only the classroom, textbook, and test, then move through life stagnate in knowledge, or study outside the class room and expand knowledge to whatever limit we desire. One must recognize that knowledge and education are vastly different.

Personal responsibility is nowhere addressed within the Constitution. Nor is it exemplified other than through responsibilities of elected officials. We have a choice to accept responsibility for our actions, or allow the government to dictate to us! Whether jobs, entitlements, or protection when we act illegally, when we delegate these responsibilities to the government, we are choosing some form of government other than a Republic based on Democratic principles!

Lawmakers too, have choices within the restraints of the Constitution. Like the population, they can choose whether to govern as a Democratic Republic, or destroy Democracy through deceit and conversion of government! "We the People," and lawmakers, still have choices today. If "we" do not make the proper choices soon, lawmakers will become totalitarian dominators! Unlike the private sector, lawmakers face as many restraints as choices.

The Founding Fathers were of many mind-sets. A compromise of those mind-sets determined a manner that provides **choices** to either live in harmony and freedom, or self-destruct as a people and nation!

If you are of the conviction the Constitution promotes evil, and politicians promote good, you are a victim of controlled education and manipulated knowledge more than Constitutional knowledge!

Never forget: Unscrupulous lawmakers depend on the voting public to "not know the difference."

The choice we have is to select honest, truthful officials who recognize and govern on the premise of "majority," or select and support those who support a specific "minority" agenda while disregarding the rights of the majority.

The Essence of Continuity of Constitution

This subject matter was specifically chosen to illustrate the following:

- The necessity of continuity of study and interpretation of the Constitution and laws of the land;
- The importance of the supporting documents;
- To demonstrate the ability of lawmakers to utilize at will, both Constitution and Articles of Federation, irrespective of the peoples wishes;
- The need of a better informed public, and a more active part in government, if Democracy, Freedom, Liberty and Justice is to prevail.

Having noted the Constitution as a guideline, a successive extension of interactive, interconnecting elements, the importance of this can be exemplified in Constitutional and legislative tenderings.

Determining the appropriate number of representatives provides an overview of interactive elements, while demonstrating the ability to misinterpret and misguide when the Constitution is compartmentalized.

Located within Article I, Section 2, Clause 3, we find the first, and misleading determinate for the number of representatives. With emphasis on subject matter, using excerpts from Clause 3, and noting "numbers" to be representative of census, we find this: "Representatives and direct taxes shall be apportioned among the several states which may be included within this union, according to their respective Numbers . . ." Farther into the paragraph, we find this: "The number of representatives shall not exceed one Representative for every thirty Thousand . . . ."

Taking the foregoing at face value, and failing to integrate with other elements of the Constitution, we readily detect a grave error. Based only on the above, and assuming one Representative per thirty thousand people, dividing the 2010 census of more than 308 Million there should be +/-10,267 members of the House. Further support of this might be argued from the Second Clause of the Fourteenth Amendment: "Representative shall be apportioned among the States according to their respective numbers, counting the whole numbers of persons in each state . . . ." No offsetting amendment is found, and the Constitution offers no direct alternative.

There is no error, but finding the conflict and determining the correct number of members, requires an integral search of relative elements. If not in the Constitution, then where is the resolution?

Interactively, clause 1, The Supremacy Clause of Article Six heavily influenced many Constitutional subjects. It is there, in part, we find resolution. More appropriately, we find a reference leading to resolution. Article Six, Clause One: "All Debts contracted and Engagements entered into, before the Adoption of this Constitution, shall be as valid against the United States under this Constitution, as under the Confederation." With emphasis on the last phrase, "as under the Confederation," we must then look to The Articles of Confederation in regards to representatives.

Article V of the Articles limits representatives in this manner: "No State shall be represented in Congress by less than two, nor more than seven members; . . ." FINALLY, we arrive at the appropriate number of Representatives, E.G., Fifty states with seven Representatives each. Or have we?

NO! By virtue of "according to the number of people" factor, that can not be correct. Census varies from state to state, and congressional district to district.

A final resolution to a total number of Representatives was established August 5, 1911 and became effective as legislated law in 1913. Public Law # 62-5 sets the number at 435 Representatives.

If in 1911 there were only 48 states, how did congress arrive at an unnatural number of 435? The answer lies in the fact that the House is composed not only of state representatives, but representatives of the respective U.S. Territories. Voting privileges are limited for the territories, but still are part of the whole number. Commonly recognized as Congressional Districts, selection of Representatives are relative to census of specific geographical areas.

The question then becomes: How can Public Law 62-5, a legislated Law, supercede the Constitution? It does not, support being found within the Supremacy Clause.

Education: Fragmenting Democracy

Education is the most influential element of any society!
In most respects, knowledge and education differ. Controlled knowledge, through manipulative education, is a danger to a Free society.

Intellectual capacity is an inherit, programmable storage facility of the mind. Information, gathered, stored and retained, becomes knowledge. Rarely, if ever, does the mind reach it fullest potential to retain knowledge. Education is the programming device by which knowledge is attained.

Education can manipulate knowledge in a variety of ways, demoting, limiting, or advancing information. Thereby education has become a major tool in the advancement of anti-American government and lifestyles!

A U.S. citizen, Presidential candidate, and devout active member of the Socialist Party once cautioned of the capabilities of education in America: "The American people will never knowingly adopt socialism. But, under the name of "liberalism," they will adopt every fragment of the socialist program, until one day America will be a socialist nation, without knowing how it happened." He continued: "I no longer need to run as a Presidential Candidate for the Socialist Party. The Democratic Party has adopted our platform!"—Norman Thomas 1948.

In the decades since his speech, expanding governmental control of educational facilities and curriculums have substantiated his dire prediction.

After five exhaustive years of research focused on Continuing Education for teachers, a Professor of Education for the University of Colorado released appalling findings. Of the several classroom situations this program addressed, the most revealing was: A **1985** High School Graduate had retained **only 75%** of the knowledge of a **1965** graduate! In the interim years, 1965-1985, the government had taken more than 90% control of education. Manipulative education in order to control knowledge.

Just as appalling are releases of 2011, when three independent studies revealed a deteriorating educational system:

- Of three-thousand, three-hundred persons surveyed, only 54% felt they understood the U.S. Constitution. Of those, only 163 political persons agree to take the survey, with only 41% indicating knowledge of the Constitution;
- As much as 75% of recent high school graduates could not name the country from which the U.S. won it's independence;
- Only 25% of all fifth graders recognized or associated with the name Abraham Lincoln
- Only 33% of participants in an online Citizenship test passed.
- The U.S. government called for more classroom hours and more school days per year, noting the U.S. lagged the world in the fields of math, science, technology, history, and government and civil affairs.

Looking back to 1965, the number of schooldays were much the same as today. With minor variances, school sessions ran from around the first week of September through late May or early June. In many agricultural areas, fall break (two weeks) around mid October allowed students to work with fall harvests. Some areas recognized a spring (planting) break as well. Holidays are much the same today as then, as are the sick-day routines. Unlike today, only minimal, if any state aid, was available. Core subjects of language, math, history, and civics (government or social studies) were mandated, while today, in many instances, they have become electives. Often, those passed over electives are major contributors to core values of adulthood! Grades were earned through application to subject matter, rather "teaching tests to meet academic minimums!" Honest hard work, family values, fiscal austerity, and the desire to become a productive citizen were the keys to education. College was something to look forward and plan for. Scholarships were Alumni or private foundations funded! Education was a step to "growing up" to adulthood! Personal and financial gains ranked second!

Although government programs disagree, those values no longer hold true for America.

From entitlement programs that assist the less fortunate, student loans, better facilities, better teacher-wages, none has escaped governmental control. Expanding Electives offer escapes from the "drudgery" while distracting from core essentials! Through controlled environments, the government continues to change an important part of knowledge as it trained new Attitudes!

Attitude defined, refined again, and controlled by incremental insertion into laws that degrades social values, disrupts family values, and defines and edits subject matter!

Fragmented Socialism! Manipulating knowledge through education!

The greatest asset, and best offense for those opposed to Freedom and Democracy is: The People don't know the difference.

Formulation and passage of Law.

Referencing the Constitution, Article I, Section 7.

Note: The difference of "Bills" and "Law" is significant. "Bill" is a term used during the formulation period. This period includes introduction, debate, voting, and passage of proposals yet to become "law." Only after passing both Houses and a Presidential signature, does a "Bill" become "law." Synonymous with law are "Act" and "Resolutions."

Common as the belief may be, the thought that Congress can not pass unconstitutional law is not factual. Albeit true that laws are to meet Constitutional authorization, too often this requirement is not met. Under the Republic form of government, Representation-by-election process, representatives may pass any law they desire. The Constitution provides for repeals, as well as amendments (modifications) when Constitutional tests fail.

In the introduction Bills, theory (Constitution) and practicality are not the same. A common misunderstanding is all Bills must originate within the House of Representatives. While bills of revenue should begin in the House, the Senate has a right to propose or concur on such bills, as with any other bill or subject of proposal.

Practically, after being presented in draft form, the house of origin will debate, change as needed, then vote. Upon acceptance, the bill will then pass to the remaining house for review. Certain subjects, such as financial appropriations and matters of defense, may be presented to respective committees for further analysis and acceptance before presentation to before the full house for debate and voting.

Interactivity between both Senate and Representative may occur several times before a mutual agreement is reached.

If both houses can not reach agreement, the bill is considered "dead" or "killed" and is set aside for future re-introduction, or perhaps, never to be revisited, depending on subject-matter.

When both houses concur with passage, the bill is then presented to the president for review and signage.

Once reaching the Executive Office, the president has ten days to act on the matter. The president can approve and sign the bill, whereby it becomes law according to a pre-determined effective date.

Should the president disprove the bill, he has two choices. He may Veto, presenting Congress (both houses) with a written explanation of disproval, or he can do nothing (known as a pocket veto).

Should a veto of either type occur, congress may then choose one of three options: 1.) Either amend the Bill as per presidential suggestion, and re-pass; or, 2.) upon mutual consent of both houses vacate (kill) the Bill entirely: or, 3.) Congress can re-pass the bill the second time. Upon second passage, the Bill becomes law, without presidential approval or signature.

Recognition and correction of Unconstitutional Law

Recognition and correction of Constitutionally Unauthorized law is a complex undertaking. Manifesting the complexity is lawmaker's belief that "The people don't know the difference." Lack of Constitutional awareness, joined with lack of financial abilities, serve to bolster to those convictions. Recognition is to be achieved only through direct and accurate understanding of the Constitution. Correction of Unconstitutional Law is yet another matter.

Corrective measures are Constitutionally defined as "due process." The costs of due process alone, allows more unconstitutional laws than any other single reason. Due process allows three methods by which laws can be Constitutionally questioned and corrected.

The most common corrective method is found when some wealthy individual, or financially supported group, files a lawsuit questioning a given law. This action normally occurs following an enforcement issue.

Law versus Regulations.

More so than passage of new laws, regulation have become an overwhelming strangulation of Freedom and Democracy. While limited regulation is necessary, unnecessary regulation has become the mantra of control and over-enlargement of government.

Regulations usually are spin-offs of some obscure, open-ended Act of Law. As Congress establishes regulatory agencies, the law is open-ended in its regulatory posture. Open-ended laws allocate Department heads, their respective advisors and committees, the authority to place whatever regulations deemed appropriate. With this posture, regulations, when committee passed, automatically become part of the existing law of subject. Having previously passed the open-ended law, no further action of congress is required.

Controversial and costly:
The Fourteenth Amendment.

No portion of the Constitution has been more controversial, or costly, than this portion of the founding document.

At the center of controversy, and exploited to the extreme, is a common belief that any person born on U.S. soil is automatically a (natural born) citizen of the U.S. Several Supreme Court decisions, as well as Legislated law, dispute this much exploited belief.

Since the date of establishment until today, the United States has recognized only two forms of citizenship, natural-born, or naturalized. Clause 1 of the 14th Amendment specifically addresses both methods. No dual-citizenship has ever been accepted by the United States.

After realizing both political power-gains, and financial advancements, lawmakers, courts, and special interest groups have chosen to deny the historical legal tenets contributing to the need, passage, and ongoing support of this amendment.

With denial at their discretion, lawmakers have implemented into the educational system denial and deletion of facts, as well as many seemly less significant, yet pertinent pieces of misinformation, while invoking and promoting damaging consequences.

At the center of argument and misinformation are two phrases, "natural born" and "jurisdiction thereof." When history is considered, the phrases are undeniably connected, explained, and undisputable in resolve to a century-old corrupted political agenda.

Prior to the amendment, and subsequent to it's ratification, various actions of states' and federal authorities indicated the need of an equitable citizenship agenda. These actions require attentiveness in order to recognize the contributions to, and cause and effects of an action such as the Fourteenth Amendment.

Setting the Stage

Long before freed slaves or repatriation of the citizens of the recent re-procurement of the Confederacy became a concern, the need of a specific protocol-for-citizenship was demonstrated. Long-standing challenges to the subject were just as needful of clarification, thus setting the stage for the Amendment.

Since early settlements, individual colonies had established treaties with local native Indian tribes. While each colony and treaty established in-colony, or intrastate agreements, they often differed in context and agreement with other colonies.

During President Andrew Jackson's administration, some thirty five years prior to the Amendment, a U.S. Supreme Court decision determined that Indian tribes were allowed to establish themselves as independent Tribal governments, or Indian Nations, conduct their affairs according to their culture and tradition, while not being subject to laws of (under the jurisdiction) the U.S. Government. Essentially, this decision established protocol and precedent of both citizenship and "jurisdiction thereof." This precedent remained intact until compromised, but not overturned, with the Immigrations Act of 1940.

In an instance of split-citizenships, E.G., Indian mother, U.S. father, no U.S. citizenship was permitted (U.S. never recognized dual citizenship) without rejection of Tribal alliance, and written application for naturalization. It is only plausible then, that children born to parents of other than U.S. citizenship, would be subject to the same merits.

Although not specifically credited as a contributor to the Amendment, an occasion of 1862 could not help but contribute to the need of a clarified method to citizenship. An abrupt about-face of ideals was demonstrated when the Supreme Court (Scott vs. The U.S. 1862) upheld slavery. This was catastrophic, leaving the Negro race without country or citizenship.

This ruling also prompted one of the most aggressive acts of ever demonstrated by a president. Following the ruling, President Lincoln issued the most profound and lasting Execitive Order in the history of this nation. The Emancipation Proclamation not only freed slaves, but bluntly proclaimed that "no nine men should rule a nation."

The Course of Events

Following the adoption of the Fourteenth Amendment, four Supreme Court cases continued support of both the "natural born" and "jurisdiction thereof" positions. Three of those cases, collectively recognized as The Slaughter-House Cases regarded citizens-of-question and their respective businesses.

The fourth, and more widely studied, is Elk vs Elkins, 1891. Elk, a Nebraska born Indian, and member of the local Indian Tribe, was refused the right to vote, based on non-citizenship status. He filed suit in federal court. The Court found that Elk was not a citizen by virtue of fact that he had neither resigned (denounced) his allegiance to the Tribal Community, nor had he applied to an authorized U.S. official, in writing, for U.S. Citizenship. Strangely, Indian Citizenship was not resolved by Congress until the Indian Citizenship Act (Snyder Act) of 1924. The Act not only recognized "Indians" as indigenous peoples, but expressly excludes other.

The residuals of those early decisions are demonstrated today, as various Indian Tribes continue to maintain their boundaries, laws, and customs, with minimal access and limited intervention of federal authority.

A U.S. Supreme Court decision of 1875 (Minor vs Happersett) clearly defined "natural born citizen." When the "natural born citizenship" eligibility for presidency was questioned, the Court determined that both parents of a natural born citizen must be U.S. Citizens.

The significance of these decisions is unquestionably conclusive:

1.) Natural Born citizenship requires U.S. citizenship of both parents;
2.) "jurisdiction there of" is not dependent upon geographical location, but that of a firmly established parental citizenship.

Collectively, these historical facts establish beyond question: citizenship is irrespective of geographical origin, being determined by parental citizenship, country or nation of origin and allegiance.

Clearly, from these early legal determinations, whether "natural born" or "naturalized citizen," an acceptable clarification of the Fourteenth Amendment is within easy reach, if resolution were sought.

Recognizable then, would be the fact that unscrupulous elected officials, and interested parties continue to defy both Constitution and Democracy, moving ever closer toward destruction of freedoms and establishment of a One-World-Government.

The Immigrations Act of 1940 compromised many previous decisions, yet did not serve to overturn them. The Act did allow the U.S. Attorney General the option of deciding on a case-by-case basis whether to prosecute, deport, or pass, on illegal entrants. This action began an open invitation to exploitation of Constitution, Law, illegals and U.S. citizens.

Under the Reagan administration, 1986 realized provisional amnesty for 3 Million plus illegals, and an attempt to establish a work program for illegals. This action further complicated the issue of immigrations and citizenship enforcement while diminishing the efforts of an already overworked Immigrations and Naturalization Agency.

In 2007 the INS was renamed Immigrations and Customs Enforcement, but exploitations of the political arena and failure to follow through by the Attorney General escalated into both enforcement and political chaos. All of which is directly associated with Clause 1 of the Amendment.

"The people don't know the difference," the greatest asset of an unscrupulous, determination-to-control form of Progressive Liberal Socialism!

Introducing The U.S. CONSTITUTION

The Constitution was adopted by a convention of the States on September 17, 1787. This text follows the copy of the Constitution signed by the authorized representatives from twelve states and General George Washington.

For reference, clauses are numbered, and changes by Amendment are enclosed in brackets followed by the respective Amendment number in parenthesis.

THE UNITED STATES CONSTITUTION

Preamble

We the People of the United States, in Order to form a more perfect Union, establish Justice, insure domestic Tranquility, provide for the common defence, promote the general Welfare, and secure the Blessings of Liberty to ourselves and our Posterity, do ordain and establish this Constitution for the United States of America.

Article I

Section 1.
The Legislature

All legislative Powers herein granted shall be vested in a Congress of the United States, which shall consist of a Senate and House of Representatives.

Section 2.
The House of Representatives.

1: The House of Representatives shall be composed of Members chosen every second Year by the People of the several States, and the Electors in each State shall have the Qualifications requisite for Electors of the most numerous Branch of the State Legislature.

2: No Person shall be a Representative who shall not have attained to the Age of twenty five Years, and been seven Years a Citizen of the United States, and who shall not, when elected, be an Inhabitant of that State in which he shall be chosen.

3: [Representatives and direct Taxes shall be apportioned among the several States which may be included within this Union, according to their respective Numbers, which shall be determined by adding to the whole Number of free Persons, including those bound to Service for a Term of Years, and excluding Indians not taxed, three fifths of all other Persons.] (14th.) The actual Enumeration shall be made within three Years after the first Meeting of the Congress of the United States, and within every subsequent Term of ten Years, in such Manner as they shall by Law direct. The Number of Representatives shall not exceed one for every thirty Thousand, but each State shall have at Least one Representative; and until such enumeration shall be made, the State of New Hampshire shall be entitled to chuse (choose) three, Massachusetts eight, Rhode-Island and Providence Plantations one, Connecticut five, New-York six, New Jersey four, Pennsylvania eight, Delaware one, Maryland six, Virginia ten, North Carolina five, South Carolina five, and Georgia three.

4: When vacancies happen in the Representation from any State, the Executive Authority thereof shall issue Writs of Election to fill such Vacancies.

5: The House of Representatives shall chuse (choose) their Speaker and other Officers; and shall have the sole Power of Impeachment.

Section 3
The Senate.

1: The Senate of the United States shall be composed of two Senators from each State, [chosen by the Legislature thereof,] (17th.) for six Years; and each Senator shall have one Vote.

2: Immediately after they shall be assembled in Consequence of the first Election, they shall be divided as equally as may be into three Classes. The Seats of the Senators of the first Class shall be vacated at the Expiration of the second Year, of the second Class at the Expiration of the fourth Year, and of the third Class at the Expiration of the sixth Year, so that one third may be chosen every second Year; [and if Vacancies happen by Resignation, or otherwise, during the Recess of the Legislature of any State, the Executive thereof may make temporary Appointments until the next Meeting of the Legislature, which shall then fill such Vacancies.] (17th)

3: No Person shall be a Senator who shall not have attained to the Age of thirty Years, and been nine Years a Citizen of the United States, and who shall not, when elected, be an Inhabitant of that State for which he shall be chosen.

4: The Vice President of the United States shall be President of the Senate, but shall have no Vote, unless they be equally divided.

5: The Senate shall chuse (choose) their other Officers, and also a President pro tempore, in the Absence of the Vice President, or when he shall exercise the Office of President of the United States.

6: The Senate shall have the sole Power to try all Impeachments. When sitting for that Purpose, they shall be on Oath or Affirmation. When the President of the United States is tried, the Chief Justice shall preside: And no Person shall be convicted without the Concurrence of two thirds of the Members present.

7: Judgment in Cases of impeachment shall not extend further than to removal from Office, and disqualification to hold and enjoy any Office of honor, Trust or Profit under the United States: but the Party convicted shall nevertheless be liable and subject to Indictment, Trial, Judgment and Punishment, according to Law.

Section 4
Elections and meetings.

1: The Times, Places and Manner of holding Elections for Senators and Representatives, shall be prescribed in each State by the Legislature thereof; but the Congress may at any time by Law make or alter such Regulations, except as to the Places of chusing (choosing) Senators.

2: The Congress shall assemble at least once in every Year, and such Meeting shall [be on the first Monday in December,] (20th) unless they shall by Law appoint a different Day.

Section 5
Adjournment, Journals, Rules, and Membership.

1: Each House shall be the Judge of the Elections, Returns and Qualifications of its own Members, and a Majority of each shall constitute a Quorum to do Business; but a smaller Number may adjourn from day to day, and may be authorized to compel the Attendance of absent Members, in such Manner, and under such Penalties as each House may provide.

2: Each House may determine the Rules of its Proceedings, punish its Members for disorderly Behaviour, and, with the Concurrence of two thirds, expel a Member.

3: Each House shall keep a Journal of its Proceedings, and from time to time publish the same, excepting such Parts as may in their Judgment require Secrecy; and the Yeas and Nays of the Members of either House on any question shall, at the Desire of one fifth of those Present, be entered on the Journal.

4: Neither House, during the Session of Congress, shall, without the Consent of the other, adjourn for more than three days, nor to any other Place than that in which the two Houses shall be sitting.

Section 6
Compensations.

1: [The Senators and Representatives shall receive a Compensation for their Services, to be ascertained by Law, and paid out of the Treasury of the United States.] (27th.) They shall in all Cases, except Treason, Felony and Breach of the Peace, be privileged from Arrest during their Attendance at the Session of their respective Houses, and in going to and returning from the same; and for any Speech or Debate in either House, they shall not be questioned in any other Place.

2: No Senator or Representative shall, during the Time for which he was elected, be appointed to any civil Office under the Authority of the United States, which shall have been created, or the Emoluments whereof shall have been encreased (increased) during such time; and no Person holding any Office under the United States, shall be a Member of either House during his Continuance in Office.

Section 7
Revenue bills, Legislative process, Presidential veto.

1: All Bills for raising Revenue shall originate in the House of Representatives; but the Senate may propose or concur with Amendments as on other Bills.

2: Every Bill which shall have passed the House of Representatives and the Senate, shall, before it become a Law, be presented to the President of the United States; If he approve he shall sign it, but if not he shall return it, with his Objections to that House in which it shall have originated, who shall enter the Objections at large on their Journal, and proceed to reconsider it. If after such Reconsideration two thirds of that House shall agree to pass the Bill, it shall be sent, together with the Objections, to the other House, by which it shall likewise be reconsidered, and if approved by two thirds of that House,

J. Monroe

it shall become a Law. But in all such Cases the Votes of both Houses shall be determined by yeas and Nays, and the Names of the Persons voting for and against the Bill shall be entered on the Journal of each House respectively. If any Bill shall not be returned by the President within ten Days (Sundays excepted) after it shall have been presented to him, the Same shall be a Law, in like Manner as if he had signed it, unless the Congress by their Adjournment prevent its Return, in which Case it shall not be a Law.

3: Every Order, Resolution, or Vote to which the Concurrence of the Senate and House of Representatives may be necessary (except on a question of Adjournment) shall be presented to the President of the United States; and before the Same shall take Effect, shall be approved by him, or being disapproved by him, shall be repassed by two thirds of the Senate and House of Representatives, according to the Rules and Limitations prescribed in the Case of a Bill.

Section 8
The powers of Congress

1: The Congress shall have Power To lay and collect Taxes, Duties, Imposts and Excises, to pay the Debts and provide for the common Defence and general Welfare of the United States; but all Duties, Imposts and Excises shall be uniform throughout the United States;

2: To borrow Money on the credit of the United States;

3: To regulate Commerce with foreign Nations, and among the several States, and with the Indian Tribes;

4: To establish an uniform Rule of Naturalization, and uniform Laws on the subject of Bankruptcies throughout the United States;

5: To coin Money, regulate the Value thereof, and of foreign Coin, and fix the Standard of Weights and Measures;

6: To provide for the Punishment of counterfeiting the Securities and current Coin of the United States;

7: To establish Post Offices and post Roads;

8: To promote the Progress of Science and useful Arts, by securing for limited Times to Authors and Inventors the exclusive Right to their respective Writings and Discoveries;

9: To constitute Tribunals inferior to the supreme Court;

10: To define and punish Piracies and Felonies committed on the high Seas, and Offences against the Law of Nations;

11: To declare War, grant Letters of Marque and Reprisal, and make Rules concerning Captures on Land and Water;

12: To raise and support Armies, but no Appropriation of Money to that Use shall be for a longer Term than two Years;

13: To provide and maintain a Navy;

14: To make Rules for the Government and Regulation of the land and naval Forces;

15: To provide for calling forth the Militia to execute the Laws of the Union, suppress Insurrections and repel Invasions;

16: To provide for organizing, arming, and disciplining, the Militia, and for governing such Part of them as may be employed in the Service of the United States, reserving to the States respectively, the Appointment of the Officers, and the Authority of training the Militia according to the discipline prescribed by Congress;

17: To exercise exclusive Legislation in all Cases whatsoever, over such District (not exceeding ten Miles square) as may, by Cession of particular States, and the Acceptance of Congress, become the Seat of the Government of the United States, and to exercise like Authority over all Places purchased by the Consent of the Legislature of the State in which the Same shall be, for the Erection of Forts, Magazines, Arsenals, dock-Yards, and other needful Buildings; And

18: To make all Laws which shall be necessary and proper for carrying into Execution the foregoing Powers, and all other Powers vested by this Constitution in the Government of the United States, or in any Department or Officer thereof.

Section 9
Limits of Congress

1: The Migration or Importation of such Persons as any of the States now existing shall think proper to admit, shall not be prohibited by the Congress prior to the Year one thousand eight hundred and eight, but a Tax or duty may be imposed on such Importation, not exceeding ten dollars for each Person.

2: The Privilege of the Writ of Habeas Corpus shall not be suspended, unless when in Cases of Rebellion or Invasion the public Safety may require it.

3: No Bill of Attainder or ex post facto Law shall be passed.

4: [No Capitation, or other direct, Tax shall be laid, unless in Proportion to the Census or Enumeration herein before directed to be taken.] (16th.)

5: No Tax or Duty shall be laid on Articles exported from any State.

6: No Preference shall be given by any Regulation of Commerce or Revenue to the Ports of one State over those of another: nor shall Vessels bound to, or from, one State, be obliged to enter, clear, or pay Duties in another.

7: No Money shall be drawn from the Treasury, but in Consequence of Appropriations made by Law; and a regular Statement and Account of the Receipts and Expenditures of all public Money shall be published from time to time.

8: No Title of Nobility shall be granted by the United States: And no Person holding any Office of Profit or Trust under them, shall, without the Consent of the Congress, accept of any present, Emolument, Office, or Title, of any kind whatever, from any King, Prince, or foreign State.

Section 10
Limitations of State Powers

1: No State shall enter into any Treaty, Alliance, or Confederation; grant Letters of Marque and Reprisal; coin Money; emit Bills of Credit; make any Thing but gold and silver Coin a Tender in Payment of Debts; pass any Bill of Attainder, ex post facto Law, or Law impairing the Obligation of Contracts, or grant any Title of Nobility.

2: No State shall, without the Consent of the Congress, lay any Imposts or Duties on Imports or Exports, except what may be absolutely necessary for executing it's inspection Laws: and the net Produce of all Duties and Imposts, laid by any State on Imports or Exports, shall be for the Use of the Treasury of the United States; and all such Laws shall be subject to the Revision and Controul (control) of the Congress.

3: No State shall, without the Consent of Congress, lay any Duty of Tonnage, keep Troops, or Ships of War in time of Peace, enter into any Agreement or Compact with another State, or with a foreign Power, or engage in War, unless actually invaded, or in such imminent Danger as will not admit of delay.

Article II
The Executive Branch

Section 1
The President

1: The executive Power shall be vested in a President of the United States of America. He shall hold his Office during the Term of four Years, and, together with the Vice President, chosen for the same Term, be elected, as follows.

2: Each State shall appoint, in such Manner as the Legislature thereof may direct, a Number of Electors, equal to the whole Number of Senators and Representatives to which the State may be entitled in the Congress: but no Senator or Representative, or Person holding an Office of Trust or Profit under the United States, shall be appointed an Elector.

3: [The Electors shall meet in their respective States, and vote by Ballot for two Persons, of whom one at least shall not be an Inhabitant of the same State with themselves. And they shall make a List of all the Persons voted for, and of the Number of Votes for each; which List they shall sign and certify, and transmit sealed to the Seat of the Government of the United States, directed to the President of the Senate. The President of the Senate shall, in the Presence of the Senate and House of Representatives, open all the Certificates, and the Votes shall then be counted. The Person having the greatest Number of Votes shall be the President, if such Number be a Majority of the whole Number of Electors appointed; and if there be more than one who have such Majority, and have an equal Number of Votes, then the House of Representatives shall immediately chuse by Ballot one of them for President; and if no Person have a Majority, then from the five highest on the List the said House shall in like Manner chuse the President. But in chusing the President, the Votes shall be taken by States, the Representation from each State having one Vote; A quorum for this Purpose shall consist of a Member or Members from two thirds of the States, and a Majority of all the States shall be necessary to a Choice. In every Case, after the Choice of the President, the Person having the greatest Number of Votes of the Electors shall be the Vice President. But if there should remain two or more who have equal Votes, the Senate shall chuse from them by Ballot the Vice President.] (12th.)

4: The Congress may determine the Time of chusing the Electors, and the Day on which they shall give their Votes; which Day shall be the same throughout the United States.

5: No Person except a natural born Citizen, or a Citizen of the United States, at the time of the Adoption of this Constitution, shall be eligible to the Office of President; neither shall any Person be eligible to that Office who shall not have attained to the Age of thirty five Years, and been fourteen Years a Resident within the United States.

6: [In Case of the Removal of the President from Office, or of his Death, Resignation, or Inability to discharge the Powers and Duties of the said Office, the Same shall devolve on the VicePresident, and the Congress may by Law provide for the Case of Removal, Death, Resignation or Inability, both of the President and Vice President, declaring what Officer shall then act as President, and such Officer shall act accordingly, until the Disability be removed, or a President shall be elected.] (20th &25th.)

7: The President shall, at stated Times, receive for his Services, a Compensation, which shall neither be encreased nor diminished during the Period for which he shall have been elected, and he shall not receive within that Period any other Emolument from the United States, or any of them.

8: Before he enter on the Execution of his Office, he shall take the following Oath or Affirmation:--â€œI do solemnly swear (or affirm) that I will faithfully execute the Office of President of the United States, and will to the best of my Ability, preserve, protect and defend the Constitution of the United States.

Section 2
Civil power of Military, Cabinet, pardon powers, and appointments.

1: The President shall be Commander in Chief of the Army and Navy of the United States, and of the Militia of the several States, when called into the actual Service of the United States; he may require the Opinion, in writing, of the principal Officer in each of the executive Departments, upon any Subject relating to the Duties of their respective Offices, and he shall have Power to grant Reprieves and Pardons for Offences against the United States, except in Cases of Impeachment.

2: He shall have Power, by and with the Advice and Consent of the Senate, to make Treaties, provided two thirds of the Senators present concur; and he shall nominate, and by and with the Advice and Consent of the Senate, shall appoint Ambassadors, other public Ministers and Consuls, Judges of the supreme Court, and all other Officers of the United States, whose Appointments are not herein otherwise provided for, and which shall be established by Law: but the Congress may by Law vest the Appointment of such inferior Officers, as they think proper, in the President alone, in the Courts of Law, or in the Heads of Departments.

3: The President shall have Power to fill up all Vacancies that may happen during the Recess of the Senate, by granting Commissions which shall expire at the End of their next Session.

Section 3
Convening Congress, and State of the Union.

He shall from time to time give to the Congress Information of the State of the Union, and recommend to their Consideration such Measures as he shall judge necessary and expedient; he may, on extraordinary Occasions, convene both Houses, or either of them, and in Case of Disagreement between them, with Respect to the Time of Adjournment, he may adjourn them to such Time as he shall think proper; he shall receive Ambassadors and other public Ministers; he shall take Care that the Laws be faithfully executed, and shall Commission all the Officers of the United States.

Section 4
Disqualification

The President, Vice President and all civil Officers of the United States, shall be removed from Office on Impeachment for, and Conviction of, Treason, Bribery, or other high Crimes and Misdemeanors.

Article III
The Judicial Branch

Section 1

The judicial Power of the United States, shall be vested in one supreme Court, and in such inferior Courts as the Congress may from time to time ordain and establish. The Judges, both of the supreme and inferior Courts, shall hold their Offices during good Behaviour, and shall, at stated Times, receive for their Services, a Compensation, which shall not be diminished during their Continuance in Office.

Section 2
Trial by jury, original jurisdiction, jury trials.

1: [The judicial Power shall extend to all Cases, in Law and Equity, arising under this Constitution, the Laws of the United States, and Treaties made, or which shall be made, under their Authority;--to all Cases affecting Ambassadors, other public Ministers and Consuls;--to all Cases of admiralty and maritime Jurisdiction;--to Controversies to which the United States shall be a Party; to Controversies between two or more States; between a State and Citizens of another State; between Citizens of different States, between Citizens of the same State claiming Lands under Grants of different States, and between a State, or the Citizens thereof, and foreign States, Citizens or Subjects.] (11th Amendment modifies entire clause.)

2: In all Cases affecting Ambassadors, other public Ministers and Consuls, and those in which a State shall be Party, the supreme Court shall have original Jurisdiction. In all the other Cases before mentioned, the supreme Court shall have appellate Jurisdiction, both as to Law and Fact, with such Exceptions, and under such Regulations as the Congress shall make.

3: The Trial of all Crimes, except in Cases of Impeachment, shall be by Jury; and such Trial shall be held in the State where the said Crimes shall have been committed; but when not committed within any State, the Trial shall be at such Place or Places as the Congress may by Law have directed.

Section 3
Treason.

1: Treason against the United States, shall consist only in levying War against them, or in adhering to their Enemies, giving them Aid and Comfort. No Person shall be convicted of Treason unless on the Testimony of two Witnesses to the same overt Act, or on Confession in open Court.

2: The Congress shall have Power to declare the Punishment of Treason, but no Attainder of Treason shall work Corruption of Blood, or Forfeiture except during the Life of the Person attainted.

Article IV
The States

Section 1
Each state to honor all others.

Full Faith and Credit shall be given in each State to the public Acts, Records, and judicial Proceedings of every other State. And the Congress may by general Laws prescribe the Manner in which such Acts, Records and Proceedings shall be proved, and the Effect thereof.

Section 2
State citizens and extradition.

1: The Citizens of each State shall be entitled to all Privileges and Immunities of Citizens in the several States.

2: A Person charged in any State with Treason, Felony, or other Crime, who shall flee from Justice, and be found in another State, shall on Demand of the executive Authority of the State from which he fled, be delivered up, to be removed to the State having Jurisdiction of the Crime.

3: [No Person held to Service or Labour (labor) in one State, under the Laws thereof, escaping into another, shall, in Consequence of any Law or Regulation therein, be discharged from such Service or Labour, but shall be delivered up on Claim of the Party to whom such Service or Labour may be due.] (13th offsets this clause.)

Section 3
New States.

1: New States may be admitted by the Congress into this Union; but no new State shall be formed or erected within the Jurisdiction of any other State; nor any State be formed by the Junction of two or more States, or Parts of States, without the Consent of the Legislatures of the States concerned as well as of the Congress.

2: The Congress shall have Power to dispose of and make all needful Rules and Regulations respecting the Territory or other Property belonging to the United States; and nothing in this Constitution shall be so construed as to Prejudice any Claims of the United States, or of any particular State.

Section 4
Republican form of Government.

The United States shall guarantee to every State in this Union a Republican Form of Government, and shall protect each of them against Invasion; and on Application of the Legislature, or of the Executive (when the Legislature cannot be convened) against domestic Violence.

Article V
Amending the Constitution, Requirements

The Congress, whenever two thirds of both Houses shall deem it necessary, shall propose Amendments to this Constitution, or, on the Application of the Legislatures of two thirds of the several States, shall call a Convention for proposing Amendments, which, in either Case, shall be valid to all Intents and Purposes, as Part of this Constitution, when ratified by the Legislatures of three fourths of the several States, or by Conventions in three fourths thereof, as the one or the other Mode of Ratification may be proposed by the Congress; Provided that no Amendment which may be made prior to the Year One thousand eight hundred and eight shall in any Manner affect the first and fourth Clauses in the Ninth Section of the first Article; and that no State, without its Consent, shall be deprived of its equal Suffrage in the Senate.

Article VI
Oaths, Debts, and Supremacy Clause.

1: All Debts contracted and Engagements entered into, before the Adoption of this Constitution, shall be as valid against the United States under this Constitution, as under the Confederation.

2: This Constitution, and the Laws of the United States which shall be made in Pursuance thereof; and all Treaties made, or which shall be made, under the Authority of the United States, shall be the supreme Law of the Land; and the Judges in every State shall be bound thereby, any Thing in the Constitution or Laws of any State to the Contrary notwithstanding.

3: The Senators and Representatives before mentioned, and the Members of the several State Legislatures, and all executive and judicial Officers, both of the United States and of the several States, shall be bound by Oath or Affirmation, to support this Constitution; but no religious Test shall ever be required as a Qualification to any Office or public Trust under the United States.

Article VII
Documents the Ratification of the Constitution

(Author's Note: Space saving warrants horizontal listing as opposed to the vertical signatures of the original document. Spelling of Signers names is unedited.)

The Ratification of the Conventions of nine States, shall be sufficient for the Establishment of this Constitution between the States so ratifying the Same. ---done in Convention by the Unanimous

Consent of the States present the Seventeenth Day of September in the Year of our Lord one thousand seven hundred and Eighty seven and of the Independence of the United States of America the Twelfth In witness whereof We have hereunto subscribed our Names.

Attest William Jackson Secretary   Go: Washington -Presidt. and deputy from Virginia.

Delaware: Geo: Read, Gunning Bedford jun, John Dickinson, Richard Bassett, Jaco Broom;

Maryland: James McHenry, Dan of St Tho Jenifer, Danl Carroll; Virginia: John Blair, James Madison Jr.; North Carolina: Wm Blount, Richd. Dobbs Spaight, Hu Williamson; South Carolina: J. Rutledge, Charles Cotesworth Pinckney, Charles Pinckney, Pierce Butler. Georgia: William Few, Abr Baldwin. New Hampshire: John Langdon, Nicholas Gilman. Massachusetts: Nathaniel Gorham, Rufus King. Connecticut: Wm. Saml. Johnson, Roger Sherman. New York: Alexander Hamilton. New Jersey: Wil. Livingston, David Brearley, Wm. Paterson, Jona. Dayton. Pennsylvania: B Franklin, Thomas Mifflin, Robt Morris, Geo. Clymer, Thos. FitzSimons, Jared Ingersoll, James Wilson, Gouv Morris.

Attest: William Jackson, Secretary.

The Amendments

No greater monument attesting the viable strength, or endurance, of both Constitution and Democratic Republic can be found than in the minimal number of changes to the Constitution. Since the establishment of the United States, its form of government, and the founding document, only twenty seven changes have made. It should be noted as found, that each of those twenty seven changes, while addressing many issues, are central to two subjects: 1.) The preservation of individual rights; and, 2.) limited scope and power of government.

When ratified in 1769, the Constitution contained no changes (Amendments.) Anticipating the need of change, The Founders set the method of change in Article V of the Constitution.

Quickly recognizing the Constitution may well allow for over expansion, erosion, and corruption of government, and diminished individual rights and freedoms, the Founders set about to extend the preservation rights and to limit size and scope of government. If individual rights and freedom were to be better preserved, and government was to be limited, immediate changes were imminent.

In the years between 1769 and 1789, several changes were proposed. Of the Twelve numbered (some went unnumbered) original proposals, ten were agreed upon and presented to Congress. On December 15, 1791, those ten changes were ratified as required in Article V., becoming a permanent part of the Constitution.

Originating as articles, these changes were renamed Amendments, and stand today as "The Bill of Rights."

The Bill of Rights, the first ten amendments, point out specific rights, allude to rights unnamed, and provide specific protection against government intervention.

Of significant importance is the difference of the Bill of Rights and other amendments. Notably, the phrase "Congress shall have power to enforce this article by appropriate legislation" is excluded from these ten amendments. Only an Amendment, not legislated law can change the provisions of the Bill of Rights.

Although few commercial publications provide insight into the importance of the Bill of Rights, or for that matter, any amendment, the Founding Fathers felt it necessary to preserve and present the importance in writing, as part of the amendments. That presentation is known as "The Preamble to the Bill of Rights," and presented herein.

Amendments of the Constitution of the United States

Preamble to the Bill of Rights

"Congress of the United States begun and held at the City of New-York, on Wednesday the fourth of March, one thousand seven hundred and eighty nine.

THE Conventions of a number of the States, having at the time of their adopting the Constitution, expressed a desire, in order to prevent misconstruction or abuse of its powers, that further declaratory and restrictive clauses should be added: And as extending the ground of public confidence in the Government, will best ensure the beneficent ends of its institution.

RESOLVED by the Senate and House of Representatives of the United States of America, in Congress assembled, two thirds of both Houses concurring, that the following Articles be proposed to the Legislatures of the several States, as amendments to the Constitution of the United States, all, or any of which Articles, when ratified by three fourths of the said Legislatures, to be valid to all intents and purposes, as part of the said Constitution; viz.

ARTICLES in addition to, and Amendment of the Constitution of the United States of America, proposed by Congress, and ratified by the Legislatures of the several States, pursuant to the fifth Article of the original Constitution."

The Bill of Rights

Amendment I
Freedom of Religion, Press, and Expression.

Congress shall make no law respecting an establishment of religion, or prohibiting the free exercise thereof; or abridging the freedom of speech, or of the press; or the right of the people peaceably to assemble, and to petition the Government for a redress of grievances.

Amendment II
Right to Bear Arms, maintain militia, security of a free state.

A well regulated Militia, being necessary to the security of a free State, the right of the people to keep and bear Arms, shall not be infringed.

Amendment III
Soldiers, quartering of.

No Soldier shall, in time of peace be quartered in any house, without the consent of the Owner, nor in time of war, but in a manner to be prescribed by law.

Amendment IV
Search and Seizure.

The right of the people to be secure in their persons, houses, papers, and effects, against unreasonable searches and seizures, shall not be violated, and no Warrants shall issue, but upon probable cause, supported by Oath or affirmation, and particularly describing the place to be searched, and the persons or things to be seized.

Amendment V
Right to Self-Protection.

No person shall be held to answer for a capital, or otherwise infamous crime, unless on a presentment or indictment of a Grand Jury, except in cases arising in the land or naval forces, or in the Militia, when in actual service in time of War or public danger; nor shall any person be subject for the same offence to be twice put in jeopardy of life or limb; nor shall be compelled in any criminal case to be a witness against himself, nor be deprived of life, liberty, or property, without due process of law; nor shall private property be taken for public use, without just compensation.

Amendment VI
Rights to speedy trial and witness confrontation.

In all criminal prosecutions, the accused shall enjoy the right to a speedy and public trial, by an impartial jury of the State and district wherein the crime shall have been committed, which district shall have been previously ascertained by law, and to be informed of the nature and cause of the accusation; to be confronted with the witnesses against him; to have compulsory process for obtaining witnesses in his favor, and to have the Assistance of Counsel for his defence.

Amendment VII
Jury Trial in Civil cases.

In Suits at common law, where the value in controversy shall exceed twenty dollars, the right of trial by jury shall be preserved, and no fact tried by a jury, shall be otherwise re-examined in any Court of the United States, than according to the rules of the common law.

Amendment VIII
Cruel and Unusual Punishment.

Excessive bail shall not be required, nor excessive fines imposed, nor cruel and unusual punishments inflicted.

Amendment IX
Prohibits denial or disparage of other rights
not specifically defined.

The enumeration in the Constitution, of certain rights, shall not be construed to deny or disparage others retained by the people.

Amendment X
Allocates power to states, and or, the people.

The powers not delegated to the United States by the Constitution, nor prohibited by it to the States, are reserved to the States respectively, or to the people.

Attest,
John Beckley, Clerk of the House of Representatives.
Sam. A. Otis Secretary of the Senate. Frederick Augustus Muhlenberg Speaker of the House of Representatives.
John Adams, Vice-President of the United States, and President of the Senate.

Amendments subsequent to the Bill of Rights

Following the 1791 ratification of the original ten amendments, only seventeen additional amendments have been accepted. The twenty-seventh, and final, ratified on May 7, 1992.

Amendment XI
Powers of Judicial.

The Judicial power of the United States shall not be construed to extend to any suit in law or equity, commenced or prosecuted against one of the United States by Citizens of another State, or by Citizens or Subjects of any Foreign State.

Amendment XII
Establishes and defines the Electoral College.

The Electors shall meet in their respective states, and vote by ballot for President and Vice-President, one of whom, at least, shall not be an inhabitant of the same state with themselves; they shall name in their ballots the person voted for as President, and in distinct ballots the person voted for as Vice-President, and they shall make distinct lists of all persons voted for as President, and of all persons voted for as Vice-President, and of the number of votes for each, which lists they shall sign and certify, and transmit sealed to the seat of the government of the United States, directed to the President of the Senate;

The President of the Senate shall, in the presence of the Senate and House of Representatives, open all the certificates and the votes shall then be counted;

The person having the greatest number of votes for President, shall be the President, if such number be a majority of the whole number of Electors appointed; and if no person have such majority, then from the persons having the highest numbers not exceeding three on the list of those voted for as President, the House of Representatives shall choose immediately, by ballot, the President. But in choosing the President, the votes shall be taken by states, the representation from each state having one vote; a quorum for this purpose shall consist of a member or members from two-thirds of the states, and a majority of all the states shall be necessary to a choice. And if the House of Representatives shall not choose a President whenever the right of choice shall devolve upon them, before the fourth day of March next following, then the Vice-President shall act as President, as in the case of the death or other constitutional disability of the President.

The person having the greatest number of votes as Vice-President, shall be the Vice-President, if such number be a majority of the whole number of Electors appointed, and if no person have a majority, then from the two highest numbers on the list, the Senate shall choose the Vice-President; a quorum for the purpose shall consist of two-thirds of the whole number of Senators, and a majority of the whole number shall be necessary to a choice. But no person constitutionally ineligible to the office of President shall be eligible to that of Vice-President of the United States.

Amendment XIII
Abolishment of Slavery.

1. Neither slavery nor involuntary servitude, except as a punishment for crime whereof the party shall have been duly convicted, shall exist within the United States, or any place subject to their jurisdiction.

2. Congress shall have power to enforce this article by appropriate legislation.

Amendment XIV
~ *The largest, and most controversial of the Amendments, this Amendment addresses four subjects: Rights of Citizenship; selection of Representative by apportionment and taxation; qualifications or disqualifications of Senators, Representatives, Presidents, and Vice-presidents; and public debt.* ~

1. All persons born or naturalized in the United States, and subject to the jurisdiction thereof, are citizens of the United States and of the State wherein they reside. No State shall make or enforce any law which shall abridge the privileges or immunities of citizens of the United States; nor shall any State deprive any person of life, liberty, or property, without due process of law; nor deny to any person within its jurisdiction the equal protection of the laws.

2. Representatives shall be apportioned among the several States according to their respective numbers, counting the whole number of persons in each State, excluding Indians not taxed. But when the right to vote at any election for the choice of electors for President and Vice President of the United States, Representatives in Congress, the Executive and Judicial officers of a State, or the members of the Legislature thereof, is denied to any of the male inhabitants of such

State, being twenty-one years of age, and citizens of the United States, or in any way abridged, except for participation in rebellion, or other crime, the basis of representation therein shall be reduced in the proportion which the number of such male citizens shall bear to the whole number of male citizens twenty-one years of age in such State.

3. No person shall be a Senator or Representative in Congress, or elector of President and Vice President, or hold any office, civil or military, under the United States, or under any State, who, having previously taken an oath, as a member of Congress, or as an officer of the United States, or as a member of any State legislature, or as an executive or judicial officer of any State, to support the Constitution of the United States, shall have engaged in insurrection or rebellion against the same, or given aid or comfort to the enemies thereof. But Congress may by a vote of two-thirds of each House, remove such disability.

4. The validity of the public debt of the United States, authorized by law, including debts incurred for payment of pensions and bounties for services in suppressing insurrection or rebellion, shall not be questioned. But neither the United States nor any State shall assume or pay any debt or obligation incurred in aid of insurrection or rebellion against the United States, or any claim for the loss or emancipation of any slave; but all such debts, obligations and claims shall be held illegal and void.

5. The Congress shall have power to enforce, by appropriate legislation, the provisions of this article.

Amendment XV
Prohibits Racial Discrimination against voters.

1. The right of citizens of the United States to vote shall not be denied or abridged by the United States or by any State on account of race, color, or previous condition of servitude.

2. The Congress shall have power to enforce this article by appropriate legislation.

Amendment XVI
Income Tax, Established and clarified.

The Congress shall have power to lay and collect taxes on incomes, from whatever source derived, without apportionment among the several States, and without regard to any census or enumeration.

Amendment XVII
Redefines method of electing Senators.

1. The Senate of the United States shall be composed of two Senators from each State, elected by the people thereof, for six years; and each Senator shall have one vote. The electors in each State shall have the qualifications requisite for electors of the most numerous branch of the State legislatures.

2. When vacancies happen in the representation of any State in the Senate, the executive authority of such State shall issue writs of election to fill such vacancies: Provided, That the legislature of any State may empower the executive thereof to make temporary appointments until the people fill the vacancies by election as the legislature may direct.

3. This amendment shall not be so construed as to affect the election or term of any Senator chosen before it becomes valid as part of the Constitution.

Amendment XVIII
Liquor Abolished ~repealed in Amendment XXI.

1. After one year from the ratification of this Amendment the manufacture, sale, or transportation of intoxicating liquors within, the importation thereof into, or the exportation thereof from the United States and all territory subject to the jurisdiction thereof for beverage purposes is hereby prohibited.

2. The Congress and the several States shall have concurrent power to enforce this Amendment by appropriate legislation.

3. This Amendment shall be inoperative unless it shall have been ratified as an amendment to the Constitution by the legislatures of the several States, as provided in the Constitution, within seven years from the date of the submission hereof to the States by the Congress.

Amendment XIX
~ Recognized as 'Women's Suffrage' this provides women the right to vote. ~

1. The right of citizens of the United States to vote shall not be denied or abridged by the United States or by any State on account of sex. Congress shall have power to enforce this Amendment by appropriate legislation.

Amendment XX
Defines terms of office for President and member of Congress.

1. The terms of the President and Vice President shall end at noon on the 20th day of January, and the terms of Senators and Representatives at noon on the 3d day of January, of the years in which such terms would have ended if this Amendment had not been ratified; and the terms of their successors shall then begin.

2. The Congress shall assemble at least once in every year, and such meeting shall begin at noon on the 3d day of January, unless they shall by law appoint a different day.

3. If, at the time fixed for the beginning of the term of the President, the President elect shall have died, the Vice President elect shall become President. If a President shall not have been chosen before the time fixed for the beginning of his term, or if the President elect shall have failed to qualify, then the Vice President elect shall act as President until a President shall have qualified; and the Congress may by law provide for the case wherein neither a President elect nor a Vice President elect shall have qualified, declaring who shall then act as President, or the manner in which one who is to act shall be selected, and such person shall act accordingly until a President or Vice President shall have qualified.

4. The Congress may by law provide for the case of the death of any of the persons from whom the House of Representatives may choose a President whenever the right of choice shall have devolved upon them, and for the case of the death of any of the persons from whom the Senate may choose a Vice President whenever the right of choice shall have devolved upon them.

5. Sections 1 and 2 shall take effect on the 15th day of October following the ratification of this Amendment.

6. This Amendment shall be inoperative unless it shall have been ratified as an amendment to the Constitution by the legislatures of three-fourths of the several States within seven years from the date of its submission.

Amendment XXI
Repeals the XVIII Amendment.

1. The eighteenth article of amendment to the Constitution of the United States is hereby repealed.

2. The transportation or importation into any State, Territory, or possession of the United States for delivery or use therein of intoxicating liquors, in violation of the laws thereof, is hereby prohibited.

3. This Amendment shall be inoperative unless it shall have been ratified as an amendment to the Constitution by conventions in the several States, as provided in the Constitution, within seven years from the date of the submission hereof to the States by the Congress.

Amendment XXII
Restricts Presidential Terms in office.

1. No person shall be elected to the office of the President more than twice, and no person who has held the office of President, or acted as President, for more than two years of a term to which some

other person was elected President shall be elected to the office of the President more than once. But this Amendment shall not apply to any person holding the office of President when this Amendment was proposed by the Congress, and shall not prevent any person who may be holding the office of President, or acting as President, during the term within which this Amendment becomes operative from holding the office of President or acting as President during the remainder of such term.

2. This Amendment shall be inoperative unless it shall have been ratified as an amendment to the Constitution by the legislatures of three-fourths of the several states within seven years from the date of its submission to the states by the Congress.

Amendment XXIII
Acquires Presidential vote for the District of Columbia.

1. The District constituting the seat of government of the United States shall appoint in such manner as the Congress may direct: A number of electors of President and Vice President equal to the whole number of Senators and Representatives in Congress to which the District would be entitled if it were a state, but in no event more than the least populous state; they shall be in addition to those appointed by the states, but they shall be considered, for the purposes of the election of President and Vice President, to be electors appointed by a state; and they shall meet in the District and perform such duties as provided by the twelfth Amendment of amendment.

2. The Congress shall have power to enforce this Amendment by appropriate legislation.

Amendment XXIV
Prohibits denial of voting rights based on taxes.

1. The right of citizens of the United States to vote in any primary or other election for President or Vice President, for electors for President or Vice President, or for Senator or Representative in

Congress, shall not be denied or abridged by the United States or any state by reason of failure to pay any poll tax or other tax.

2. The Congress shall have power to enforce this Amendment by appropriate legislation.

Amendment XXV
Sets forth procedures for mid-term presidential successor.

1. In case of the removal of the President from office or of his death or resignation, the Vice President shall become President.

2. Whenever there is a vacancy in the office of the Vice President, the President shall nominate a Vice President who shall take office upon confirmation by a majority vote of both Houses of Congress.

3. Whenever the President transmits to the President pro tempore of the Senate and the Speaker of the House of Representatives his written declaration that he is unable to discharge the powers and duties of his office, and until he transmits to them a written declaration to the contrary, such powers and duties shall be discharged by the Vice President as Acting President.

4. Whenever the Vice President and a majority of either the principal officers of the executive departments or of such other body as Congress may by law provide, transmit to the President pro tempore of the Senate and the Speaker of the House of Representatives their written declaration that the President is unable to discharge the powers and duties of his office, the Vice President shall immediately assume the powers and duties of the office as Acting President. Thereafter, when the President transmits to the President pro tempore of the Senate and the Speaker of the House of Representatives his written declaration that no inability exists, he shall resume the powers and duties of his office unless the Vice President and a majority of either the principal officers of the executive department or of such other body as Congress may by law provide, transmit within four days to the President pro tempore of the Senate and the Speaker of the House of Representatives their written declaration that the President

is unable to discharge the powers and duties of his office. Thereupon Congress shall decide the issue, assembling within forty-eight hours for that purpose if not in session. If the Congress, within twenty-one days after receipt of the latter written declaration, or, if Congress is not in session, within twenty-one days after Congress is required to assemble, determines by two-thirds vote of both Houses that the President is unable to discharge the powers and duties of his office, the Vice President shall continue to discharge the same as Acting President; otherwise, the President shall resume the powers and duties of his office.

Amendment XXVI
Voting age changed to 18.

1. The right of citizens of the United States, who are 18 years of age or older, to vote, shall not be denied or abridged by the United States or any state on account of age.

2. The Congress shall have the power to enforce this Amendment by appropriate legislation.

Amendment XXVII
Realignment of Compensation to Congressional Members.

No law varying the compensation for the services of the Senators and Representatives shall take effect until an election of Representatives shall have intervened.

The Declaration of Independence

It behooves the citizens of modern day United States to observe the several accusations launched against the King of England regarding treatment of the new North American colonies, then compare to the advanced control and over-enlargement of the present-day U.S. Government.

The Unanimous Declaration of the Thirteen United States of America.

When, in the course of human events, it becomes necessary for one people to dissolve the Political Bands which have connected them with another, and to assume among the Powers of the Earth, the separate and equal Station to which the Laws of Nature and of Nature's God entitle them, a decent Respect to the Opinions of Mankind requires that they should declare the causes which impel them to the Separation.

We hold these Truths to be self-evident, that all Men are created equal, that they are endowed by their Creator with certain unalienable Rights, that among these are Life, Liberty and the Pursuit of Happiness. That to secure these Rights, Governments are instituted among Men, deriving their just Powers from the Consent of the Governed, that whenever any Form of Government becomes destructive to these Ends, it is the Right of the People to alter or to abolish it, and to institute new Government, laying its Foundation on such Principles and organizing its Powers in such Form, as to them shall seem most likely to effect their Safety and Happiness. Prudence, indeed, will dictate that Governments long established should not be hanged for light and transient Causes; and accordingly all Experience hath shown that Mankind are more disposed to suffer, while Evils are sufferable, than to right themselves by abolishing the Forms to which they are accustomed. But when a long Train of Abuses and Usurpations, pursuing invariably the same Object, evinces a Design to reduce them under absolute Despotism, it is their Right, it is their Duty, to throw off such Government, and to provide new Guards for their future Security.Such has been the patient Sufferance of these Colonies; and such is now the Necessity which constrains them to alter their former Systems of Government. The History of the present King of Great Britain is a History of repeated Injuries and Usurpations, all having in direct object the Establishment of an absolute Tyranny over these States. To prove this, let Facts be submitted to a candid World.

HE has refused his Assent to Laws, the most wholesome and necessary for the public good.

HE has forbidden his Governors to pass Laws of immediate and pressing Importance, unless suspended in their Operation till his Assent should be obtained; and when so suspended, he has utterly neglected to attend to them.

HE has refused to pass other Laws for the Accommodation of large Districts of People, unless those People would relinquish the Right of Representation in the Legislature, a Right inestimable to them and formidable to Tyrants only.

HE has called together Legislative Bodies at Places unusual, uncomfortable, and distant from the Depository of their public Records, for the sole Purpose of fatiguing them into Compliance with his Measures.

HE has dissolved Representative Houses repeatedly, for opposing with manly Firmness his Invasions on the Rights of the People.

HE has refused for a long Time, after such Dissolutions, to cause others to be elected; whereby the Legislative Powers, incapable of Annihilation, have returned to the People at large for their exercise; the State remaining in the meantime exposed to all the Dangers of Invasion from without, and the Convulsions within.

HE has endeavored to prevent the Population of these States; for that Purpose obstructing the Laws for Naturalization of Foreigners;

refusing to pass others to encourage their Migration hither, and raising the Conditions of new Appropriations of Lands.

HE has obstructed the Administration of Justice, by refusing his Assent to Laws for establishing Judiciary Powers.

HE has made Judges dependent on his Will alone, for the Tenure of their Offices, and the Amount and Payment of their Salaries.

HE has erected a Multitude of new Offices, and sent hither Swarms of Officers to harass our People, and eat out their Substance.

HE has kept among us, in Times of Peace, Standing Armies without the consent of our Legislature.

HE has affected to render the Military independent of and superior to Civil Power.

HE has combined with others to subject us to a Jurisdiction foreign to our Constitution, and unacknowledged by our Laws; giving his Assent to their Acts of pretended Legislation: FOR quartering large Bodies of Armed Troops among us: FOR protecting them, by mock Trial, from Punishment for any Murders which they should commit on the Inhabitants of these States: FOR cutting off our Trade with all Parts of the World: FOR imposing Taxes on us without our Consent: FOR depriving us in many Cases, of the Benefits of Trial by Jury: FOR transporting us beyond Seas to be tried for pretended Offences: FOR abolishing the free System of English Laws in a neighboring Province, establishing therein an arbitrary Government, and enlarging its Boundaries so as to render it at once an Example and fit Instrument for introducing the same absolute Rule into these Colonies: FOR taking away our Charters, abolishing our most valuable Laws, and altering fundamentally the Forms of our Governments: FOR suspending our own Legislatures, and declaring themselves invested with Power to legislate for us in all Cases whatsoever.

HE has abdicated Government here, by declaring us out of his Protection and waging War against us.

HE has plundered our Seas, ravaged our Coasts, burned our Towns, and destroyed the Lives of our People.

HE is, at this Time, transporting large Armies of foreign Mercenaries to compleat the Works of Death, Desolation, and Tyranny, already begun with circumstances of Cruelty and Perfidy,

J. Monroe

scarcely paralleled in the most barbarous Ages, and totally unworthy the Head of a civilized Nation.

HE has constrained our fellow Citizens taken Captive on the high Seas to bear Arms against their Country, to become the Executioners of their Friends and Brethren, or to fall themselves by their Hands.

HE has excited domestic Insurrections amongst us, and has endeavored to bring on the Inhabitants of our frontiers, the merciless Indian Savages, whose known Rule of Warfare, is undistinguished Destruction of all Ages, Sexes and Conditions.

IN every stage of these Oppressions we have Petitioned for Redress in the most humble Terms: Our repeated Petitions have been answered only by repeated Injury. A Prince, whose Character is thus marked by every act which may define a Tyrant, is unfit to be the Ruler of a free People.

NOR have we been wanting in Attentions to our British Brethren. We have warned them from Time to Time of attempts by their Legislature to extend an unwarrantable Jurisdiction over us. We have reminded them of the Circumstances of our Emigration and Settlement here. We have appealed to their native Justice and Magnanimity, and we have conjured them by the Ties of our common Kindred to disavow these Usurpations, which, would inevitably interrupt our Connections and Correspondence. They too have been deaf to the Voice of Justice and Consanguinity. We must, therefore, acquiesce in the Necessity, which denounces our Separation, and hold them, as we hold the rest of Mankind, Enemies in War, in Peace, Friends.

WE, therefore, the Representatives of the UNITED STATES of AMERICA, in General Congress, Assembled, appealing to the Supreme Judge of the World for the Rectitude of our Intentions, do, in the Name, and by the Authority of the good People of these Colonies, solemnly Publish and Declare, that these United Colonies are, and of Right ought to be, FREE AND INDEPENDENT STATES; that they are absolved from all Allegiance to the British Crown, and that all political Connection between them and the State of Great Britain, is and ought to be totally dissolved; and that as FREE AND INDEPENDENT STATES, they have full Power to levy War, conclude Peace, contract Alliances, establish Commerce, and to do all other Acts and Things which INDEPENDENT STATES may of right do.

And for the support of this Declaration, with a firm Reliance on the Protection of Divine Providence, we mutually pledge to each other our Lives, our Fortunes, and our sacred Honor.

Signers:

New Hampshire: Josiah Bartlett, William Whipple, Matthew Thornton

Massachusetts: John Hancock, Samual Adams, John Adams, Robert Treat Paine, Elbridge Gerry Rhode Island: Stephen Hopkins, William Ellery

Connecticut: Roger Sherman, Samuel Huntington, William Williams, Oliver Wolcott

New York: William Floyd, Philip Livingston, Francis Lewis, Lewis Morris

New Jersey: Richard Stockton, John Witherspoon, Francis Hopkinson, John Hart, Abraham Clark Pennsylvania: Robert Morris, Benjamin Rush, Benjamin Franklin, John Morton, George Clymer, James Smith, George Taylor, James Wilson, George Ross

Delaware: Caesar Rodney, George Read, Thomas McKean

Maryland: Samuel Chase, William Paca, Thomas Stone, Charles Carroll of Carrollton

Virginia: George Wythe, Richard Henry Lee, Thomas Jefferson, Benjamin Harrison, Thomas Nelson, Jr., Francis Lightfoot Lee, Carter Braxton

North Carolina: William Hooper, Joseph Hewes, John Penn

South Carolina: Edward Rutledge, Thomas Heyward, Jr., Thomas Lynch, Jr., Arthur Middleton Georgia: Button Gwinnett, Lyman Hall, George Walton.

Signed July 4, 1776 in Philadelphia, Pa. A copy was not presented to England until 1782.

The First Constitution

Established by the thirteen original colonies (states), and considered to be the first U. S. Constitution, the Articles of Confederation were agreed upon on November 15, 1777, yet ratification did not occur until March 5, 1781. Like the Declaration of Independence, much of it's contents were refined, rewritten, then incorporated into the final document, the current Constitution.

The Articles of Confederation was formed and ratified by the states of New Hampshire, Massachusetts-bay Rhode Island and Providence Plantations, Connecticut, New York, New Jersey, Pennsylvania, Delaware, Maryland, Virginia, North Carolina, South Carolina and Georgia.

The Articles of Confederation

ARTICLE I
The Stile of this Confederacy shall be "The United States of America". (Author's note: "Stile" as used herein refers to steps, or methods and mannerisms by which issues are addressed and accomplished.

ARTICLE II
Each state retains its sovereignty, freedom, and independence, and every power, jurisdiction, and right, which is not by this Confederation expressly delegated to the United States, in Congress assembled.

ARTICLE III
The said States hereby severally enter into a firm league of friendship with each other, for their common defense, the security of their

liberties, and their mutual and general welfare, binding themselves to assist each other, against all force offered to, or attacks made upon them, or any of them, on account of religion, sovereignty, trade, or any other pretense whatever.

ARTICLE IV

The better to secure and perpetuate mutual friendship and intercourse among the people of the different States in this Union, the free inhabitants of each of these States, paupers, vagabonds, and fugitives from justice excepted, shall be entitled to all privileges and immunities of free citizens in the several States; and the people of each State shall free ingress and regress to and from any other State, and shall enjoy therein all the privileges of trade and commerce, subject to the same duties, impositions, and restrictions as the inhabitants thereof respectively, provided that such restrictions shall not extend so far as to prevent the removal of property imported into any State, to any other State, of which the owner is an inhabitant; provided also that no imposition, duties or restriction shall be laid by any State, on the property of the United States, or either of them.

If any person guilty of, or charged with, treason, felony, or other high misdemeanor in any State, shall flee from justice, and be found in any of the United States, he shall, upon demand of the Governor or executive power of the State from which he fled, be delivered up and removed to the State having jurisdiction of his offense.

Full faith and credit shall be given in each of these States to the records, acts, and judicial proceedings of the courts and magistrates of every other State.

ARTICLE V

For the most convenient management of the general interests of the United States, delegates shall be annually appointed in such manner as the legislatures of each State shall direct, to meet in Congress on the first Monday in November, in every year, with a power reserved to each State to recall its delegates, or any of them, at any time within the year, and to send others in their stead for the remainder of the year.

No State shall be represented in Congress by less than two, nor more than seven members; and no person shall be capable of being a delegate for more than three years in any term of six years; nor shall any person, being a delegate, be capable of holding any office under the United States, for which he, or another for his benefit, receives any salary, fees or emolument of any kind.

Each State shall maintain its own delegates in a meeting of the States, and while they act as members of the committee of the States.

In determining questions in the United States in Congress assembled, each State shall have one vote.

Freedom of speech and debate in Congress shall not be impeached or questioned in any court or place out of Congress, and the members of Congress shall be protected in their persons from arrests or imprisonments, during the time of their going to and from, and attendence on Congress, except for treason, felony, or breach of the peace.

ARTICLE VI

No State, without the consent of the United States in Congress assembled, shall send any embassy to, or receive any embassy from, or enter into any conference, agreement, alliance or treaty with any King, Prince or State; nor shall any person holding any office of profit or trust under the United States, or any of them, accept any present, emolument, office or title of any kind whatever from any King, Prince or foreign State; nor shall the United States in Congress assembled, or any of them, grant any title of nobility.

No two or more States shall enter into any treaty, Confederation or alliance whatever between them, without the consent of the United States in Congress assembled, specifying accurately the purposes for which the same is to be entered into, and how long it shall continue.

No State shall lay any imposts or duties, which may interfere with any stipulations in treaties, entered into by the United States in Congress assembled, with any King, Prince or State, in pursuance of any treaties already proposed by Congress, to the courts of France and Spain.

No vessel of war shall be kept up in time of peace by any State, except such number only, as shall be deemed necessary by the United States in Congress assembled, for the defense of such State, or its trade; nor shall any body of forces be kept up by any State in time of peace, except such number only, as in the judgement of the United States in Congress assembled, shall be deemed requisite to garrison the forts necessary for the defense of such State; but every State shall always keep up a well-regulated and disciplined militia, sufficiently armed and accoutered, and shall provide and constantly have ready for use, in public stores, a due number of filed pieces and tents, and a proper quantity of arms, ammunition and camp equipage.

No State shall engage in any war without the consent of the United States in Congress assembled, unless such State be actually invaded by enemies, or shall have received certain advice of a resolution being formed by some nation of Indians to invade such State, and the danger is so imminent as not to admit of a delay till the United States in Congress assembled can be consulted; nor shall any State grant commissions to any ships or vessels of war, nor letters of marque or reprisal, except it be after a declaration of war by the United States in Congress assembled, and then only against the Kingdom or State and the subjects thereof, against which war has been so declared, and under such regulations as shall be established by the United States in Congress assembled, unless such State be infested by pirates, in which case vessels of war may be fitted out for that occasion, and kept so long as the danger shall continue, or until the United States in Congress assembled shall determine otherwise.

ARTICLE VII.

When land forces are raised by any State for the common defense, all officers of or under the rank of colonel, shall be appointed by the legislature of each State respectively, by whom such forces shall be raised, or in such manner as such State shall direct, and all vacancies shall be filled up by the State which first made the appointment.

ARTICLE VIII.

All charges of war, and all other expenses that shall be incurred for the common defense or general welfare, and allowed by the United States in Congress assembled, shall be defrayed out of a common treasury, which shall be supplied by the several States in proportion to the value of all land within each State, granted or surveyed for any person, as such land and the buildings and improvements thereon shall be estimated according to such mode as the United States in Congress assembled, shall from time to time direct and appoint.

The taxes for paying that proportion shall be laid and levied by the authority and direction of the legislatures of the several States within the time agreed upon by the United States in Congress assembled.

ARTICLE IX.

The United States in Congress assembled, shall have the sole and exclusive right and power of determining on peace and war, except in the cases mentioned in the sixth article —of sending and receiving ambassadors —entering into treaties and alliances, provided that no treaty of commerce shall be made whereby the legislative power of the respective States shall be restrained from imposing such imposts and duties on foreigners, as their own people are subjected to, or from prohibiting the exportation or importation of any species of goods or commodities whatsoever —of establishing rules for deciding in all cases, what captures on land or water shall be legal, and in what manner prizes taken by land or naval forces in the service of the United States shall be divided or appropriated — of granting letters of marque and reprisal in times of peace —appointing courts for the trial of piracies and felonies commited on the high seas and establishing courts for receiving and determining finally appeals in all cases of captures, provided that no member of Congress shall be appointed a judge of any of the said courts.

The United States in Congress assembled shall also be the last resort on appeal in all disputes and differences now subsisting or that hereafter may arise between two or more States concerning boundary, jurisdiction or any other causes whatever; which authority shall always be exercised in the manner following. Whenever the legislative or executive authority or lawful agent of any State in controversy with another shall present a petition to Congress stating the matter in question and praying for a hearing, notice thereof shall be given by order of Congress to the legislative or executive authority of the other State in controversy, and a day assigned for the appearance of the parties by their lawful agents, who shall then be directed to appoint by joint consent, commissioners or judges to constitute a court for hearing and determining the matter in question: but if they cannot agree, Congress shall name three persons out of each of the United States, and from the list of such persons each party shall alternately strike out one, the petitioners beginning, until the number shall be reduced to thirteen; and from that number not less than seven, nor more than nine names as Congress shall direct, shall in the presence of Congress be drawn out by lot, and the persons whose names shall be so drawn or any five of them, shall be commissioners or judges, to hear and finally determine the controversy, so always as a major part of the judges who shall hear the cause shall agree in the determination: and if either party shall neglect to attend at the day appointed, without showing reasons, which Congress shall judge sufficient, or being present shall refuse to strike, the Congress shall proceed to nominate three persons out of each State, and the secretary of Congress shall strike in behalf of such party absent or refusing; and the judgement and sentence of the court to be appointed, in the manner before prescribed, shall be final and conclusive; and if any of the parties shall refuse to submit to the authority of such court, or to appear or defend their claim or cause, the court shall nevertheless proceed to pronounce sentence, or judgement, which shall in like manner be final and decisive, the judgement or sentence and other proceedings being in either case transmitted to Congress, and lodged among the acts of Congress for the security of the parties concerned: provided that every commissioner, before he sits in judgement, shall take an oath to be administered by one of the judges of the supreme or superior court of the State, where the cause shall be tried, 'well and truly to hear and determine the matter in question, according to the best of his judgement, without favor, affection or hope of reward': provided also, that no State shall be deprived of territory for the benefit of the United States.

All controversies concerning the private right of soil claimed under different grants of two or more States, whose jurisdictions as they may respect such lands, and the States which passed such grants are adjusted, the said grants or either of them being at the same time claimed to have originated antecedent to such settlement of jurisdiction, shall on the petition of either party to the Congressof the United States, be finally determined as near as may be in the same manner as is before presecribed for deciding disputes respecting territorial jurisdiction between different States.

The United States in Congress assembled shall also have the sole and exclusive right and power of regulating the alloy and value of coin struck by their own authority, or by that of the respective States —fixing the standards of weights and measures throughout the United States —regulating the trade and managing all affairs with the Indians, not members of any of the States, provided that the legislative right of any State within its own limits be not infringed or violated -- establishing or regulating post offices from one State to another, throughout all the United States, and exacting such postage on the papers passing through the same as may be requisite to defray the expenses of the said office —appointing all officers of the land forces, in the service of the United States, excepting regimental officers —appointing all the officers of the naval forces, and commissioning all officers whatever in the service of the United States —making rules for the government and regulation of the said land and naval forces, and directing their operations.

The United States in Congress assembled shall have authority to appoint a committee, to sit in the recess of Congress, to be denominated 'A Committee of the States', and to consist of one delegate from each State; and to appoint such other committees and civil officers as may be necessary for managing the general affairs of the United States under their direction —to appoint one of their members to preside, provided that no person be allowed to serve in the office of president more than one year in any term of three years; to ascertain the necessary sums of money to be raised for the service of the United States, and to appropriate and apply the same for defraying the public expenses —to borrow money, or emit bills on the credit of the United States, transmitting every half-year to the respective States an account of the sums of money so borrowed or emitted —to build and equip a navy —to agree upon the number of land forces, and to make requisitions from each State for its quota, in proportion to the number of white inhabitants in such State; which requisition shall be binding, and thereupon the legislature of each State shall appoint the regimental officers, raise the men and cloath, arm and equip them in a solid-like manner, at the expense of the United States; and the officers and men so cloathed, armed and equipped shall march to the place appointed, and within the time agreed on by the United States in Congress assembled. But if the United States in Congress assembled shall, on consideration of circumstances judge proper that any State should not raise men, or should raise a smaller number of men than the quota thereof, such extra number shall be raised, officered, cloathed, armed and equipped in the same manner as the quota of each State, unless the legislature of such State shall judge that such extra number cannot be safely spread out in the same, in which case they shall raise, officer, cloath, arm and equip as many of such extra number as they judeg can be safely spared. And the officers and men so cloathed, armed, and equipped, shall march to the place appointed, and within the time agreed on by the United States in Congress assembled.

The United States in Congress assembled shall never engage in a war, nor grant letters of marque or reprisal in time of peace, nor enter into any treaties or alliances, nor coin money, nor regulate the value thereof, nor ascertain the sums and expenses necessary for the defense and welfare of the United States, or any of them, nor emit bills, nor borrow money on the credit of the United States, nor appropriate money, nor agree upon the number of vessels of war, to be built or purchased, or the number of land or sea forces to be raised, nor appoint a commander in chief of the army or navy, unless nine States assent to the same: nor shall a question on any other point, except for adjourning from day to day be determined, unless by the votes of the majority of the United States in Congress assembled.

The Congress of the United States shall have power to adjourn to any time within the year, and to any place within the United States, so that no period of adjournment be for a longer duration than the space of six months, and shall publish the journal of their proceedings monthly, except such parts thereof relating to treaties, alliances or military operations, as in their judgement require secrecy; and the yeas and nays of the delegates of each State on any question shall be entered on the journal, when it is desired by any delegates of a State, or any of them, at his or their request shall be furnished with a transcript of the said journal, except such parts as are above excepted, to lay before the legislatures of the several States.

ARTICLE X.

The Committee of the States, or any nine of them, shall be authorized to execute, in the recess of Congress, such of the powers of Congress as the United States in Congress assembled, by the consent of the nine States, shall from time to time think expedient to vest them with; provided that no power be delegated to the said Committee, for the exercise of which, by the Articles of Confederation, the voice of nine States in the Congress of the United States assembled be requisite.

ARTICLE XI.
Canada acceding to this confederation, and adjoining in the measures of the United States, shall be admitted into, and entitled to all the advantages of this Union; but no other colony shall be admitted into the same, unless such admission be agreed to by nine States.

ARTICLE XII.
All bills of credit emitted, monies borrowed, and debts contracted by, or under the authority of Congress, before the assembling of the United States, in pursuance of the present confederation, shall be deemed and considered as a charge against the United States, for payment and satisfaction whereof the said United States, and the public faith are hereby solemnly pleged.

ARTICLE XIII.
Every State shall abide by the determination of the United States in Congress assembled, on all questions which by this confederation are submitted to them. And the Articles of this Confederation shall be inviolably observed by every State, and the Union shall be perpetual; nor shall any alteration at any time hereafter be made in any of them; unless such alteration be agreed to in a Congress of the United States, and be afterwards confirmed by the legislatures of every State.

Recommended Readings and References

- The Federalist Papers
- The Jeffersonian Papers and Archives
- Archives of each of the Founding Fathers
- The Citizens Guide—Offers a variety of subjects relative to government
- Culture of Corruption—Michelle Malken
- Crimes against Liberty—David Limbaugh
- Throw Them All Out—Peter Schweizer

For Comparative analysis:
- The Communist Manifesto
- The Constitution of any non-democratic nation.